2/12

CR

WHAT DOES IT DO?
COMBINE

BY MARK FRIEDMAN

Published in the United States of America by Cherry Lake Publishing
Ann Arbor, Michigan
www.cherrylakepublishing.com

Content Adviser: Louis Teel, Professor of Heavy Equipment, Central Arizona College

Photo Credits: Cover and page 1, ©Kletr/Shutterstock, Inc.; page 5,
©Daniele Silva/Shutterstock, Inc.; page 7, ©iofoto/Shutterstock, Inc.; page 9,
©Hisom Silviu/Shutterstock, Inc.; page 11, ©Pierre BRYE/Alamy;
page 13, ©iStockphoto.com/Elenathewise; page 15, ©sima/
Shutterstock, Inc.; page 17, ©Jan van Broekhoven/Shutterstock, Inc.; page 19,
©smart.art/Shutterstock, Inc.; page 21, ©Cultura/Alamy

LIBRARY OF CONGRESS CATALOGING-IN-PUBLICATION DATA
Friedman, Mark, 1963-
  What does it do? Combine/by Mark Friedman.
    p. cm.—(Community connections)
  Includes bibliographical references and index.
  ISBN-13: 978-1-61080-117-1 (lib. bdg.)
  ISBN-10: 1-61080-117-2 (lib. bdg.)
  1. Combines (Agricultural machinery) I. Title. II. Title: Combine.
  S696.F75 2011
  633.1'045—dc22   2011000258

Cherry Lake Publishing would like to acknowledge the
work of The Partnership for 21st Century Skills. Please
visit www.21stcenturyskills.org for more information.

Printed in the United States of America
Corporate Graphics Inc.
July 2011
CLFA09

COMBINE

CONTENTS

WHAT DOES IT DO?

WHAT IS A COMBINE?

Have you ever wondered how farmers **harvest** the crops in their fields? One machine does most of the work. It is called a **combine**.

Farmers drive combines through rows of crops that are ready to be picked.

It would take farmers a long time to harvest their crops without the help of combines.

A combine does many different jobs. First, the combine **reaps**. That means it cuts the plants from the ground.

Then it **threshes** them. This is when the grain is separated from the rest of the plant.

Finally, the combine unloads the grain. It also gets rid of the rest of the plant.

A farmer carefully drives a combine through his fields.

MAKE A GUESS!

The combine got its name because it combines many jobs into one. These jobs used to be done separately. Why might farmers want to use a machine that combines many jobs?

7

REAPING

A combine's first job is to reap the plants. This is done by the **header** at the front of the combine. It gathers the plants into bunches. These bunches are pushed back into the combine.

The header helps make sure plants are cut in neat rows.

Look at the header. It makes sure each row of crops is cut evenly. The farmer has to steer the combine carefully so it can cover every row in the field.

9

The bunches of plants end up at the cutter bar. The cutter bar looks like big scissors. It chops the plants from the ground.

The cutter bar is very close to the ground. This helps it cut the plants down low near the dirt. A **conveyor** moves the cut plants deeper into the combine.

The cutter bar cuts plants down low to the ground.

THRESHING

The conveyor brings the plants to the **threshing drum**. Bars in the drum beat the stalks. This shakes the grains or seeds loose.

The grains are the parts of the plant that we eat. The rest of the plant is either **straw** or **chaff**.

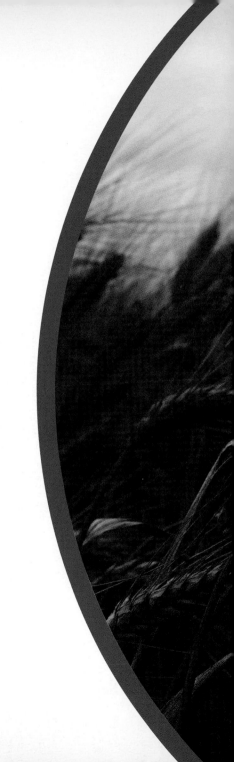

The threshing bar separates the grains from the rest of the plant.

13

The grains fall down after they come loose. They collect in a tank under the threshing drum.

Another conveyor takes the straw and chaff toward the back of the combine. They are beaten again along the way. This knocks any extra grains down into the tank.

Grains are only a small part of each plant.

Grains or seeds fall downward in the threshing drum. Straw and chaff do not. Why do you think this is?

FINISHING THE PROCESS

A combine can only hold so much grain at once. But farmers don't want to stop working to empty their combines. So a tractor drives next to the combine. The grain is collected in a trailer pulled by the tractor.

Tractors and trailers are used for many jobs on a farm.

First, grain travels up an elevator in the combine. Then it shoots out of the combine through a pipe. The grain lands in the trailer.

A worker drives the trailer back to the farm. He unloads the grain into a storage bin. Then he returns to the field to collect more grain from the combine.

A combine was used to fill this trailer with sunflower seeds.

19

What happens to the straw and chaff? The combine takes care of that, too! Some combines spread them around to cover the field.

Other combines have a machine that ties the straw into bundles. Farmers use the straw bundles for animal bedding. No part of the plant goes to waste. And the great combine does all the work!

It is important to follow safety rules when using a combine.

Do you know anyone who works on a farm? Ask about safety rules for using combines. These big machines can be dangerous if they are not used the right way!

21

GLOSSARY

chaff (CHAF) husks, leaves, and other parts of a plant that people don't eat

combine (KAHM-bine) a harvesting machine that performs several different jobs as it moves over a field

conveyor (kuhn-VAY-ur) a machine that moves objects from one place to another

harvest (HAR-vist) to pick crops when they are ripe

header (HED-ur) the device at the front of the combine that gathers and cuts the crops

reaps (REEPS) cuts down plants

straw (STRAW) dried stems of plants such as wheat

threshes (THRESH-iz) beats plants to separate the grain from the straw and chaff

threshing drum (THRESH-eeng DRUM) the part of a combine that separates the grain from the straw and chaff

22

FIND OUT MORE

BOOKS

Alexander, Heather. *Big Book of Tractors*. New York: DK Publishing, 2007.

Pipe, Jim. *Farm Machines*. Mankato, MN: Stargazer Books, 2009.

WEB SITES

Agriculture in the Classroom

agclassroom.org/kids/index.htm
Try some fun science experiments related to farms.

Farmers' Museum: Harvest of History
www.harvestofhistory.org/
Learn how crops were harvested before combines were invented.

John Deere Kids' Corner
www.deere.com/en_US/compinfo/kidscorner/home.html
Play games and learn more about farm machines.

INDEX

ABOUT THE AUTHOR

Mark Friedman has been a writer and editor of children's books and educational materials for 20 years. He has written picture books, biographies, textbooks, and books on science concepts, history, culture, government, poetry, holidays, religion, and more.